T0072597

STORY OF THE SOUL

STORY OF THE SOUL

Akhtar Naveed Syed

PARTRIDGE
A Penguin Random House Company

ISBN: Softcover   978-1-4828-2768-2
               eBook   978-1-4828-2769-9

To order additional copies of this book, contact
Toll Free 800 101 2657 (Singapore)
Toll Free 1 800 81 7340 (Malaysia)
orders.singapore@partridgepublishing.com

www.partridgepublishing.com/singapore

CONTENTS

DEDICATION:

To my father, Syed Jalaluddin, and my mother, Anjum Jalal who have nurtured me and helped me believe in myself.

ACKNOWLEDGEMENTS:

My elder brother, Farhat Nasir Syed, helped me realize when to actually share my deepest feelings with the world.

My wife, Aniqa Bano, who has constantly shown me the path to be myself in the real world.

My niece, Sarah Syed, who gave me the confidence to go through the publication of this work.

1. AN ODE TO MY SOULMATE

Your head is blank

You don't have any feelings

All feelings are from heaven

But heaven is lost lost in the deep ocean

The oceans are beneath the seas yet the seas
themselves are beneath the oceans

The sea and the ocean are entangled to form a web

The spider forming the web is in my heart

My heart is soulless, my soul is mindless yet
who brought me to this is unknown

What is known is that I sold my heart to the seas

The mermaids make me insane yet my insanity is my ecstasy

What am I to do — my heart is burning, my
soul is bursting, my brain is melting

My demons drown me but my soul fights on in futility till the dawn

What is the dawn?

It is the resurrection of my soul

2. FACES ARE ENTRAPMENTS

Entrapments are the heart's snares

Endless strands of rays of hope

Strains of which enrich the soul

Power of these magnets is endless

Intense resonance pulls souls together

A stare is like a peak

A peak that is akin to a horizon

The view's alchemy steals hearts

The alchemy is the varied expressions

Faces are these soul-to-soul cupids

3. PIGEONS

Heaven's animals whose fate is unknown

Fate is a destiny whose cause is an enigma

The mystery of this phenomenon is known to all

However, the animals are too innocent to know

The birds' naivety predestines them to fail

This failure is a sorry tale

A tale whose tail is all curled up

The entanglements leave the birds to have nightmares

The dreams scare them to death

4. SCARECROWS

Humans made of straw

Shapes made of sunrays

Visions, which scare birds

Birds, which love to prey

Yet the predator becomes the prey

The predator is the flimsiest beast

The beasts are horrified by the sight

The sight is a dark shadow emanating rays of black magic

The magic's magician tricks the birds through a masked covering

The real prey dances with joy

The tricked and disillusioned beings hope death is near

Yet there's no death

All is well

It's just a matter of perception

The predators are blind

The fate of the blind is always being totally utterly deceived

5. THE SEAFARING PORPOISE

A messenger of hope, pleasure, fun, frolic and a merfolk

A being termed as saviour of the oceans

Oceans being his home

His companion being the mermaid queen

A queen who is his mistress, soul mate

The porpoise lives somewhere nowhere everywhere
except where his life's essence lives

Endlessly he looks for the one and only sweetheart
who resides in his heart soul and mind

The queen drifts in all times yet her mate is nowhere
but her soul knows he is very near

The porpoise lives in the Azores

The queen lives in the Indian Ocean

Their cupid resides in the Gulf of Oman

Their altar is at the cheetah's house

The cheetah awaits them with no worry for he is a fortune teller

6. THE KAZAKH FAIRY

A fairy whose beauty is mesmerising

She waits for her lover

The lover lives near Xiangi

The era is 1180A.D.

The two have never seen heard each other

They meet one another in their dreams

Their meeting place is Al Farabi's school of philosophy

The dreams are real

They hold arms kiss touch and feel each other

In real life they're melancholically drifting nowhere

One is a fortune teller on the road to Taklamakan Desert

The other lives near the fairies' lake

The lover is a dimension drifter

Al Farabi is their teacher, cupid and best friend

The fairy and the lover lie forever in bliss

Yet they dream in today's world

7. A WHALE'S EYE VIEW

The sea is as blue as the azure sky

The sky the sea floor

The rocks are the air

The air is in the water

The water is my home

My home is 10 nautical miles from The Cook Islands

The isles' are pristine

The untouched landmass welcomes all on its shore

The shore calls all beings to dance

The voodoo dancers set the rhythm

The ocean's rhythm is total brotherhood

My heart goes out to the soul sisters

The sisters are Anna, Maria, Firdosa

The seagull tells them where to find their lovers

Their lovers are Duncan, Marriot, Peter

They live 50 leagues under the sky

Near the Mariana Trench

8. THE FIRE BREATHING DRAGON

Fire is life

Life is hot cold molten frozen

The dragon is a sweet angel

The angel is a sweet radiant glowing source of light

The light takes my breath away

My breath smells of the succulent pieces of grass

Our charming dragon turned the tables

The fellow met his mate in the seas

The seas are their home

Their home is my home

But their home is miles away

Forever Mr & Mrs Dragon live peacefully

Their peace is never disturbed

Whoever tries melts

Hurrah for the great dragon

9. THE SEA SNAKE COUPLE AT PONAPE

The land of beautiful squids, octopus and ray fishes

Beings, which are harmless

The nearby sea snakes scare them

Yet Rosie and Ramdas have no idea why

The two never leave each other

They are soul mates forever

Have said that they have lost each other

Their mothers have been scared senseless

However, they reappear as if they were there forever

Their fathers knew all that

Thus they played with two jellyfishes

Rosie and Ramdas have no brothers no sisters yet they have five friends

Morn, Torn, Worn, Sorn, Dron are the five lucky seahorses

The sea snakes and the sea snakes love each other

The planktons are jealous, but who cares

10. THE SERENE BEACHES OF SEYCHELLES

As I saw the beach I was mesmerised

The view left me stunned

The schools of fish brought me to ecstasy

My ecstasy is soul deep

The jellyfish played voodoo music

Music, which was like heaven's harp

The harp was played by the breathtaking fairy

The fairy's eyes were scorching red

It blinded the blinded souls but brought sheer
joy to the souls without holes

The fairy hugged me forever

I will love her forever

I will miss her forever

I will yearn for her forever

I hope she will reciprocate

My wish is to go to the altar with her

Hope that we will be soul mates, playmates forever

11. THE ZAMBIAN TORTOISE

Is this a sea being from heaven?

No it may be a bird from paradise

The cat sniffed it

The 'pussy cat' hooted at it

The nightly stars stared at it

The papa bear knew what it was

The mama bear did too

And so did the big bear

Yet the baby bear couldn't believe what he was seeing

To him it was a Lilliputian gargoyle

A gargoyle that brought smiles to everyone's faces

All the faces lit up

All the lit up faces brimmed with joy

Their joy was destroyed when the angelic being disappeared

While disappearing it made no noise

Yet the 'pussy cat'

The cat was told but it too small to understand

12. THE MINSTREL OF SPAIN

My best friend since our times immemorial

He showed me Spain

It rendered no pain

Yet I felt saddened to the core

This mate of mine will and is with me forever

He is the best pest yet I am his pest

His being there is a surety

My being there is a rarity

However, my rarity is as good as his surety

What is good for him is good for me too

He has always shown me the way

His is the right way

For he follows the right path

As he is the minstrel of Madrid

His strange musings are my whisperings

All this is understood by no one

And I hope no one ever will

Yet our inheritors are staking their claim on the treasure chest

13. A PARAKEET'S MESSAGE

This is my best friend

Yet I could not save him from death

The cat ate him while I fought with the cat

But in my dreams he called

I was astonished for he did not admonish me

He just wanted me to meet his pal

I was afraid that his pal was a predator too

I tried unashamedly to stay away from his friend

However, in the end I had to meet him

He turned out to be an old friend of mine

Yet I did not recognise him

Only the parakeet told me he was my friend

When I went into a coma the clarity hit

Its glare sent me into a frenzy

In my mind I met this friend of mine

Who like me was in a coma too

Yet it was a meeting of minds

Now I don't want anything to change till eternity ends

14. TYPES OF GOATS

What are goats?

They are nothing but oats

What kinds of oats are they?

Both the worst and the best

They eat grass and fish in the same gulp

The fish eaters are the sea-goats

They work for the mermaids

The mermaids are their mistresses

These mermaids live in solitude

Hoping for the goats to bring a mate

But these goats are worthless

All they do is munch planktons

Even the planktons cry at the goat's misdemeanour

Yet the goats remain unashamed

However, the mermaids love these goats

For they provide them company

Which they yearn forever till time seizes

Yet if time seizes how will the goats breathe again

15. MESSENGERS OF FATES

Fates are soul's prisons

Prisons, which mar people's destinies

Destinies, which are lost forever

Even forever is a short time

For the forever is shortened by fates' messengers

These messengers live in heaven

Heaven is from where they observe all

As they are worthy angels

These angels help the soulless and the gutless

Those are those who have lost their souls forever

Till they are met by these angels

Angels, which help every soul except the dark ones

The dark souls destroy these angels

Their deeds are very good

The soulless souls thank them forever

16. FATELESS GUPPIES

Birds with no minds

But not mindless minds

The depth of their thoughts is intense

The intensity scares all the birds

Yet, being a humming bird, I feel no fear

The eagles and the vultures shy away from them

Their shyness is the cause

Their hearts have no fear

These guppies are not real birds

They are the sea's birds

They swim with octopus and sea anemones

No bird ever sees them

Except the kingfisher and the seagulls

These two nourish on the poor guppies

Yet if they were birds they would have been devoured by eagles and foxes

Being fishes is a small price to pay

As being in sea creature's intestines they still smell the briny air

17. TRAGEDIES ARE CUNNING

What is cunning?

Life is that

How can tragedies hurt one's heart?

By simple experiences

The cunning life cares for no one

Not a soul

All are left helpless

These helpless souls pray for a better life

Yet life is ever torturous

The torture tears minds

Such minds succumb to pressures

Pressures which are strange and mind boggling

Their strangeness causes the tenseness

No one is able to cope with them

All feel vanquished

Such is the defeat of the cunning tragedies

In this victory is the defeat of itself

All this exists only in my mind

18. A BEAR'S CRY

A soul deep cry of the wild

Not from the wild west but the east

It is an eastern howl

The sound, which sends chills down spines

But in the east it's the sound you dream to hear

This is so in the east as well as the north

The people in shark skins respect

The igloo dwellers think of them as teachers

One may ask who are they

They are whiter than snow

Are pinker than flamingos

Swim faster than sea dwellers

Come to think of it they are in the west too

They are the kings of the Arctic

Their presence brings an angel on the tundra land

The Eskimo keeps him as a pet

They posses a shrill cry for which his mate lusts after

19. THE EVIL WITHIN MANKIND

Mankind is truly sickening

I wish I was a spiritual being

A being, which stays in hearts, souls and all empty spaces

This evil burns my core

A core, which is so scarred that you cannot see the real face

The evil succumbs all people to become evil

This causes people to become nasty

All nastiness is unhamanly

Yet all mankind is nasty at times

What can be done?

Nothing it seems

Except waiting, hoping, praying that this evil disappears

However, this is no chance of that happening

As this evil is truly satanic

This virtue spoils mankind

One hopes it will disappear one day

20. A HEARTLESS SWORD

A swordfish's sword

Not heartless at all

Yet all fishermen think it as heartless

The sword is not a weapon

It is nothing but an instrument

It helps the maligned fish to hunt

The cries are heard by all

All fishes stay away from the swordfish

Though this fish loves all sea animals

It's a kind fish

It never pokes anyone with its probing sword

Yet no one likes it

Why would they like this sword?

Because of its innovativeness

No that too is a figment of imagination

All is all this sword is truly heartless

As it loves killing beings

21. A MINDBLOWING ROMANCE

The lovers are two whales

One lives in the Pacific

The other in the Arctic

Both know each other by letters exchanged

The letters are delivered by sonar mail

Their cupid is a flock of seagulls

The whole group transfers millions of mails daily

Both the whales are love struck

One of them decides to swim over

The passage takes her a week

Yet on reaching she finds he has left to find her

The sonar got jumbled

The whale swims back

On half way back the whales meet each other

Now they can't decide where to live

So they decide to meet a sage

The sage is bewildered too

He tells them it would be better leave one another

22. THE DANCING WITCHES

A tea meeting of out of this world

The tea served by two witches

One was a mermaid, the other a fairy

Both bewitched my core

Both talked to me telepathically

Each was conveying to me a message

My conscious became my unconscious

My dreams became my realities

All three of us were on such a carpet

A truly wondrous carpet

The wonder was how easily we were meeting mentally

The witches have friends

They are fairies

They, too, bewitched me

The fairies are my godmothers

So is the elder witch

The mermaid is my dream

But now my dreams are my dreams

23. THE BEAUTIES OF THE URALS

People ask me where are the Urals

Who knows I say

They look up the map of the Americas and can't find them there

I have a gig

For I went to the place 5,000 years ago

It was a campsite

The camp was of a circus

The circus had a theatre

The theatre had actresses, actors

The actresses were all beauties

I was the muse of these beauties

I helped them fall in love

Bringing sweet desires in their minds

Teasing their souls

Making them realise their men's desires

They could never thank me

For I died a moth's death

24. THE RUSSIAN SEDUCTRESS

She was of my friend's

My friend was her lover

Their love was great

She was this seductress

She had to tease and please him

Yet he never moved

He never fell in love

She tried, tried all in vain

He was my friend

He fell betrayed

For he thought she was my lover

He thought I fooled him

She too fell betrayed

They started to cast an evil spell

Yet they fell in love with each other

Now I became an evil cupid

However, I was his best man and her maid of honour

For all of us are earthworms

25. THE KING OF CUPIDS

Who are the cupids of this world?

Are they men, hen or women?

Do they live in pens or dens?

No to all

They live in nests

Do their work in the air

They are the lovely seagulls

In the water and the air they share their work

The land cupids are the owls

The water cupids are the sea anemones .

Together they are magnificent cupids

However the king is the seagull

They plan it all

Hire the muses

Tame the beauties

Civilise the males

They have horns and spikes

Their lovers need muses too

26. THE SNOW LEOPARD OF KARACHI

Karachi is my hometown

So is it of my playmate

My playmate is a pigmy snow leopard

She lived with me for 50 years

I am a small ginger cat

The years are cat years

Both of us are still friends

She has gone on to heaven

But the fairies tell me of her

She was such a mean, lean, killing machine

She ate rats and I ate mice

She loved hunting hens and I parrots

Her friend was a black panther

Both of them played hide and seek

I was afraid of the panther

She was the panther's friend forever

Her master was a prince

A shrewd prince who loved her deeply

27. THE QUEEN OF BELLY DANCERS

She is a beauty from Corsica

Her dance is so exquisite

Her moves are mesmerising

All dancers try to ape her

Her complex renderings bewitch all

She is from a village

She loved moving her feet since age 1

Her father sent her to a dance coach on Barbary Island

The teacher was a good dancer

This queen lives 3,000 years from now

Her island is better than most places

Her students roam the world

Her fellow dancers, too, love her dance

She has hundreds of suitors

None please her

She desperately needs a muse and cupid

She now has found them

Yet she is yet to find her lover

28. THE EAST EUROPEAN ANGELS

These are five angels

They belong to the house of serpents

All five of them are exquisite pieces of beauty

Scores of men fancy them

Four are blondes, one is a black top

They'd love to have men too

As till now they have not gone to the altar

They are dancers in Taklamakan desert's oasis town

They travelled from Blaj in Romania

The Mongol horsemen and Chinese in caravans loved their dance

Of these angels one is my true love

I love her deeply

She knows this

But we still live apart

Our love is known to all five

Their teacher is between me and her

29. THE WARRIOR CHARIOT

This is Harriet's chariot

But who is Harriet?

She is an elf's maid

They live deep in the forest

The forest is enchanted

Gnomes also live there

Harriet is one of them

She helps soldiers of all sides

She rides on her chariot

Her horses are real stallions

She is the best nurse

She is perfect at her work

All sides laud her

Her chariot is irreparable now

She is inconsolable

She fell down broke her ribs

Her whole tale is so sorrowful

As she is at her death bed

30. THE DREAM MACHINE

A machine, which knows no bounds

Which passes through time

Passes through realms

All of which are real yet imaginary

The machine is everywhere

One uses it at sleep

When one awakens it shuts off

That's what life is all about

This machine nourishes

It replenishes souls

What if it always stayed on?

The dreams would be endless

So endless that there will be no realty

All reality would disappear

We would need no food and drinks

Yet some live their dreams

What if they could live their realities?

All will be different yet nothing will be different

31. THE SORCERER'S REVENGE

Who takes revenge?

Only a beast

What constitutes a beast?

Nothing but a body full of hate and conceit

What good is such a body?

Totally nothing

Yet, the sorcerer is right to take revenge

He is a humble sorcerer

His magic is a boon for all

I am under his spell

I am a tricked sea anemone

To get cured I am under his spell

He is not a monster as most think

He pleases me a lot

He used his powers on a fellow sea anemone

We are no more friends

She tried to kill me by a wizard's magic

I am thankful to the mighty sorcerer

32. THE HONEST LIAR

A liar who shares his soul

A soul, which meddles with everyone's lives

All are uneasy by his thoughts

The thoughts are unnerving and beguiling

However, he is a saint

He does all this in ignorance and innocence

Yet all blame him for this treachery

He is helpless

Yet he continues with his unadmirable ways

A seagull tries to tame him

She lures him to her nest

A nest full of eggs for him to care

However, he continues his ways

Showing her no respect

The liar is vanquished by a witch

He now turns into a sweet angel

33. THE PERSIAN PRINCESS

A princess with wings

Wings as beautiful as a peacock's

Her hair are golden

Her skin is dead white

She seduces no one

She gets seduced by no one

Her dreams tell her who her lover is

The lover too dreams of her

They live thousands of miles away

And they live in 5,000BC and 5,000AD

So how can they meet?

Except in their dreams

A doctor shows her the way

But the cure is useless

There is no cure

Only that the princess becomes a fairy

34. A TYRANT'S MURDER

Who murders who

A tyrant another tyrant

What's the use?

None

Really

Yes

No not at all

They both think they are right

Yet both are wrong

Both are sinful

Should go to hell

Though even hell will vomit them

They killed their souls

Now they are just agents of dark forces

They both plead innocence

But both will be punished equally

35. THE MUSLIN CLOTH

A cloth that holds life

As life ebbs away

My life is going away

I have no one to save me

Yet this tells me to hold on

That I do with utmost ease

The cloth is a family heirloom

It has saved endless souls

All souls are now in ecstasy

The cloth always hangs by the balcony

The balcony of the family's tomb

No one is afraid of it

Except Satan

He wants to have people murder themselves

But the heavenly cloth saves them

36. A DOLPHIN'S CRY FOR HELP

Help is in the saviour's hands

Hands, which are nine feet wide

The width engulfs all sorrows

The dolphin is helpless

Waiting for the whale of his dreams

His dreams are never fulfilled

Yet his dream whale swims in wait

His cry is an SOS

The call is that he seeks his whale

The whale is sure

What if she proposes?

Will the shy dolphin refuse?

She can't be sure

So she turns to a cupid

The cupid is a bird-cat of the sea

That is a sea-lioness

37. THE HELPLESS PRISONER

A prisoner who has lost his head

The headless person waits for his soul to depart

Yet that's taking time

Maybe the soul thinks the head will be reattached

A heavenly fairy comes to rescue the soul

The soul cries its heart out

The fairy and her pals dance around the head

Somehow the head is not detached

It was just a cut in the thread

The fairies are pleased to tell this to the soul

The prisoner wakes up but he has now lost his soul

It seems the soul has gone on a trip

A trip that may cost the prisoner's life

A life that may soon end

Yet the soul comes back within seconds

The prisoner's mind is thankful to the soul

38. THE MICROSCOPIC PLANETS

Planets in the head

The atoms of the soul

The electrons of the mind

The photons of the brain

They all are matter

They all rotate

All transform into energy

Energy that connects

The connection transfers souls

To the next stop

The brain to work

The mind to think

But do they exist

Sure they do

Otherwise what would be the point of living

These planets are real heavenly bodies

39. THE STARS THAT EVOKE DREAMS

Dreams that scare people

Tear their hearts into two

People who think too much

Thinking that breaks the dreams

Stars that bind the soul with the mind

The beauty of the stars befuddle all

Send people into a trance

Their naivety appeals to people

But that's the core of their beauty

Their thoughts please many

Most want to think like

But can't, as their hearts are blackened

Yet they cry for the star' attention

40. THE VOICE WITHIN

A soul deep voice

The voice of my heart

A heart, which has been crushed

The source of this torture is no one but another voice

That is my mind's voice

This voice suspends my soul

My soul yearns for my heart's voice

A voice to which all listen

My soul yearns for my heart's voice

A voice, which alarms me and even others

Both voices are my own

However, my self loves the mind's voice

For it's the sensible one

My soul is an irrational being

Thus it loves my heart's voice

A being, which is totally fanciful

41. THE MYSTERY OF THE SAINTS

These are the saints of paradise

They are angels of that habitat

They guide the mortal souls

They follow the commandments unquestionably

Their job is to guard paradise

The paradise is my ecstasy

This ecstasy can always be harmed by dark deeds and beings

These saints are my pals

They are in reality my thoughts

The rationale behind my decisions

Without them I would be nowhere

No, nowhere too would be somewhere

I would be in a bottomless pit

A pit inhabited by satanic beings

The mystery is only mine to know

42. MESSENGER OF DEATH

Death will come

Its messenger will bring it

This messenger is nothing but a feeling

A feeling from the heavens

A heart-felt notion

That makes one believe his fate

I already feel it

The feeling I feel is out of this world

It's a notion

Some fairies are calling

I once gave them my soul

They want me back

Yet I am stuck here

Here is my life

There is my death

43. THE HEARTLESS FOX

Not a sly fox

But a deadly fox

A fox who lives in the alleys of hell

A hellish being who has the vampire's habit

Even the vampire will be frightened by him

His heartlessness is famed

However the fame is of being murderous

Endless souls have been turned to dust by him

His end will come

His progeny will destroy him

They feel the hurt of the others

The fox knows this all

Yet he continues his merry ways

His ways are as satanic as Satan's

His fate is being tortured for him

Life is not enough, an eternity is!

44. CHAINS OF EMOTIONS

My emotions hurt me

The hurt is felt to my core

My core burns

The burning scars my soul

My scarred soul cries for help

Help comes from a Mauritanian beauty

Her eyes swell my heart

Her gaze un-scar my soul

My core finds a reason to live

Then she disappears

Yet she leaves behind in me a feeling to live on

However, I see she is there peeking from behind the cliff

Her presence is a gift for me

Her memories drive me on

Its nothing but a turn of emotions

45. A CRY FOR HELP BY THE WOMEN IN THE DUNGEON

Who are these women?

They are prisoners of their fate

They live in their heart's dungeons

Their dungeons are their prisons

Prisons, which force them to have no feelings

In their unconscious they cry for help

No one listens to these cries except the fairies

The fairies prey for these women

The women are my classmates

My stares imprisoned them

They lost feeling when I tricked them and conned them

The fairies know this

So they had me trapped by the queen

The queen is an evil mermaid

But one that is suitable for the heartless merfolk

46. A TIGER'S TAIL

A ten feet long tail

A tiger with a spider monkey's face

A spider monkey with a cheetah's fur

A tail with a tale of his own

No this is not a chimera

It is an Indian cheetah

Caught by the tail

By an uncle of mine

Who only saw the cat's tail

Maybe the tail was a piece of cloth

For I never saw it

Anyway, he kept it in his cupboard

So it has to be a cloth piece

No but he swore it was a tiger's tail

Sorry, I forget if it's a tiger or a cheetah

Anyway it will remain a mysterious tale

47. THE SAVIOUR OF THE DEATHS

Who is this saviour?

He is the dolphin of the poles

He helps men, porpoise and all other sea creatures

A small dolphin with a big heart

A heart that saves souls from murders

The murderers are the ships

Ships of oils and pesticides

The deaths are of planktons, fishes and sharks

The dolphin needs the help of the seafaring porpoise

They together help these souls

However, both of them look for their mermaids

Their mermaids, too, are helper creatures

All such beings are the saviours

The beneficiaries pray for them

They only want to save more lives

48. COMRADES IN ARMS

Three dear friends holding hands in hand

All swam and played by the sea

The sea shells pricked

They did not mind that

For them it was acupuncture

As they frolicked the dolphins swam by

They were fascinated

They were mystified

Seeing this the dolphins jumped with joy

They look like flying fish

The comrades were left stunned

Their astonishment made the sea laugh

The laughter of the waves made the buddies shudder

In their frightened state they returned to their golden chariots

49. THE PURPLE PRIEST

A Levi priest

A true saint

Who lives in Ethiopia

But is not his homeland

His homeland is between Baghdad and Cairo

The Coptics despise his tribe

Yet they prosper

In their success they belittle all

This treachery angers all

However, in the parallel universe where I live
in they are not Levis but just crows

This universe is ours

The crows, too, are despised

In cities they abound

Where they belittle the other birds

Birds with mindblowing whistles

50. THE SEDUCTRESS AND HER SLAVE

The slave is an ape

The mistress is his slave

Her slavery knows no mounds

The bounds limits' are so wide

The width lets them discover each other

The seductress is the mistress

The slave brings offerings to this goddess of his

The goddess continues to tease him

He loves to be teased

For he is so enraptured by her spell

No she is not a witch

Yet her magic brings peace to his heart

She is a chimp who has ensnared this ape

This ape loves his fate

51. THE SERENE HORDE

A horde so beautiful

Yet so miserable

All the members are depressed

This depression is felt by all

Yet their keeper sees that they stay like this

This misery is not a misery

It is a misery with a twist

A twist, which enchants the hordes

They feed on particles in the sand

With a vengeance seen in no beast

All beasts are envious of them

But their jealousy does not bother these sweet gargoyles

These angelic beings are beautiful to watch

52. THE SPRINGS OF NEVADA

Is it Nevada or Adaven?

Adaven sounds funky

This land is near the Mariana Trench

From where the Barbarry pirates reach the oldest world

This is the one Jules Verne discovered

All laughed at this suggestion

Yet this Duke Barbosa is the commander of that land

Where sea monsters abound

Dinosaurs talk to manatees

Ostriches make love to dodos

Here all women have light coloured eyes

For they are witches

Witches who have stolen Barbosa's heart

Who is so so in love

The springs here are of pure white milk

53. THE SUPERSONIC ANGELS

A beacon in the sky

The sky reaching to the seventh heaven

It lighted when I reached the gate of hell

Where the enchantress' island lies

The island is where I was born

My birth was scary as hell was near

But our tribe of seducers is used to that

Through these angels we connect with others of our tribe

They all live in other galaxies

We all are the keepers of the underworld

Which is guarded by the Amazonias of Deccan

They are fairies

Back on earth to defend the universe

Or is it a multiverse?

54. THE WATERY GRAVE

Where is this?

Is it the Noah's floods deads' remains

No, it's the remnants of a storm

A storm that hit paradise

A paradise in the sky

Which leads to Atlantis

The tombs are of the angels, fairies and troll who guard this path

Who initiated this storm?

A demon who is in league with satan

Now this land has been replenished

Can one control these forces of darkness?

By seeking the charmed ones in Mu

Where is Mu?

Somewhere in the Pacific Ocean

55. A SIREN'S PRISONER

Prisoner of her soul

Soul of a siren

Siren so bewitching

Her sight entrances all

All who despise her

All who love her

She is a witch

A witch of the seas

A sea where the prisoner lives

Her prisoner is a merman

A being who loves her

Yet she tortures him

A practice he loves

His heart is hers

She gives him her virginity

A state so divine

A divinity he steals

Now he wishes to worship her

She teases him endlessly

He loves the feeling

56. MERMAIDS OF MY DREAMS

Dreams made in heaven

Heaven made of water

Water in the sky

Sky on the ground

Ground so high above

A place so serene

A serenity of sirens

Sirens that I love

Love of the mermaids

Mermaids who possess me

An ownership I cherish

A pleasure so resounding

Yet I never dream

The dreams are of a siren

A siren of paradise

The paradise where I live

Life full of pleasure

Pleasure the mermaids seek

The mermaids are my soul mates

Mates who are in my dreams

57. LOVERS OF MY DREAMS

Lovers who love to tease

A teasing that I love

Yet I never find love

Love that is in my dreams

Dreams that I see

The vision is in my dreams

Yet I am awake

An awakening so comatose

A slumber, which I love

A love full of lovers

Lovers who are sirens

Sirens who are goddesses

I am their slave

A slave for eternity

A time in my dreams

Dreams that never end

An ending that never comes

Yet I wait

A waiting so short

Pleasured by the lovers

58. MERMAIDS OF INDUS

A river so pure

A purity so divine

Divinity that houses goddesses

Goddesses that are virgins

Virginity so pristine

A wildness so seductive

Seduction of the sirens

Sirens worshipped by the dolphins

Dolphins so blind

Men who love the sirens

Sirens tease them

Sirens are hated

Men lose their souls

Souls so dark

Darkness hated by the sirens

Sirens of my existence

They are my mates

Mates whom I worship

For I am a dolphin

A being so in awe of the sirens

59. MERMAIDS OF CASPIAN

A sea of my vision

Vision that I see

A sight in my hallucination

My brain in a trance

An affect of the sirens

Sirens of the sea

Sea so salty

The sirens love the salt

Salt that they relish in

Men are so afraid of them

They lose their souls to them

Souls so devious

The sirens so pure

A purity felt by the salmons

Salmons who are their slaves

Slaves who worship them

They ensnare the men

Men who are the devil's incarnate

An existence so hideous

A fact hated by the mermaids

60. MERMAIDS OF MY LIFE

Life as a slave

Slave of serenes

Serenes so seductive

A seduction so pleasing

A pleasure I seek

Serenes that ensnare me

An entrapment so divine

A feeling so mesmerising

An existence so loving

A love of the serenes

Who are my mates

Mates so sweet

Who are my goddesses

Goddesses whom I worship

They are my life's purpose

Purpose so nice

An existence so soothing

A feeling the sirens love

Love shared by me

For I am so in a trance by their ways

61. MY ENCHANTING DREAMS

Dreams sent by fairies

Fairies of Thiarca

Thiarca of Homer

Homer in my dream

Dreams so so enchanting

A spell so entrancing

Fairies whom I seek

I am besotted by one of them

The fairies visit me

My dreams are so vivid

A clarity that brings ecstasy

A feeling so refreshing

An awakening so intense

An intensity so heart felt

The fairy is a mermaid

A siren so serene

Her serenity allures me

A seduction in dreams

Dreams I see endlessly

Yet she is never there

62. PARADISE OF MY DREAMS

Dreams sent by mermaids

Mermaids to whom I am enslaved

A slavery so worthwhile

I am so ecstatic

A feeling so cherishing

The joy I see in my dreams

Dreams made in paradise

Paradise full of mermaids

Mermaids whom I love

A love so intense

Whose strength is so endearing

My pleasures are endless

The paradise is my home

Home where I live

A life full of dreams

Dreams of my soul mates

Mates who are mermaids

Creatures so divine

I savour their matriarchy

Yet I yearn to reach this paradise

63. THE GODDESS SIREN

A siren from Siberia

Siberia in heaven

A being so beautiful

Beauty in the eyes

Eyes so green

A colour of the witch

Her eyes frighten all

Yet some are seduced by her

A feeling they love

Her shape is so divine

Her worshippers love to please her

A pleasure she loves

Her subjects love her appearance

An appearance from heaven

She being a goddess

A goddess of the world

World she created

A creation loved by all

She loves to tease all

All who love her ways

64. THE MERMAID'S LOVER

A lover who is a water being

A being so sweet

A sweetness so innocent

An innocence the mermaid loves

A love he loves

Their love blossoms

Fruits are shared

They reach ecstasy

Yet he despises her

For she loves others

Others whom she treasures

She loves to tease him

He hates her

Yet she pleases him

Her lovers are all mermaids

Mermaids so treacherous

He is scared of them

They too seduce him

He becomes their lover

His mate now imprisons his soul

65. THE WICKED MERMAIDS

Sirens of hell

Hell that is their prison

Prison of lava

Lava so hot

Hell they love

Love so soul deep

Souls so impure

Dirt so deep

Depth so scary

A sight hated by all

Their ways so devious

Yet they're so sweet

The beings of hell love them

They worship them

For they are their goddesses

Goddesses of fire

Fire of devil's existence

Existence so heart breaking

A sight so breathtaking

A feeling so unnerving

66. POSERS ARE HYPOCRITES

Hypocrites of thoughts

Thoughts of actions

Actions concealed

Concealed as in veiled

Veiled by slyness

Slyness that poses

Poses to be true

Truth that is false

False as a poser

Poser as a freethinker

Thinking not

Not as in human

Human that is closed

Closed as a path

Path that are his thoughts

67. FEAR OF FEAR

Fear of thoughts

Thoughts that unnerve

Unnerve my mind

Mind full of ideas

Ideas of passion

Passion for a cause

Cause for a struggle

Struggle of mankind

Mankind in need of my ideas

Ideas for sharing

Sharing to bring change

Change that many fear

Fear that must be erased